Special thanks to Gillian Morris for making this songbook happen

Transcribed by Danny Begelman

Project Manager: Carol Cuellar
Music Editor: Colgan Bryan
Book Art Layout: Joe Klucar
Album Art: © 2003 Wind-up Entertainment, Inc.
Photography: Frank Veronsky

BRING ME TO LIFE

Written by Ben Moody,
Amy Lee and David Hodges

Moderately ♩ = 96
Intro:

6

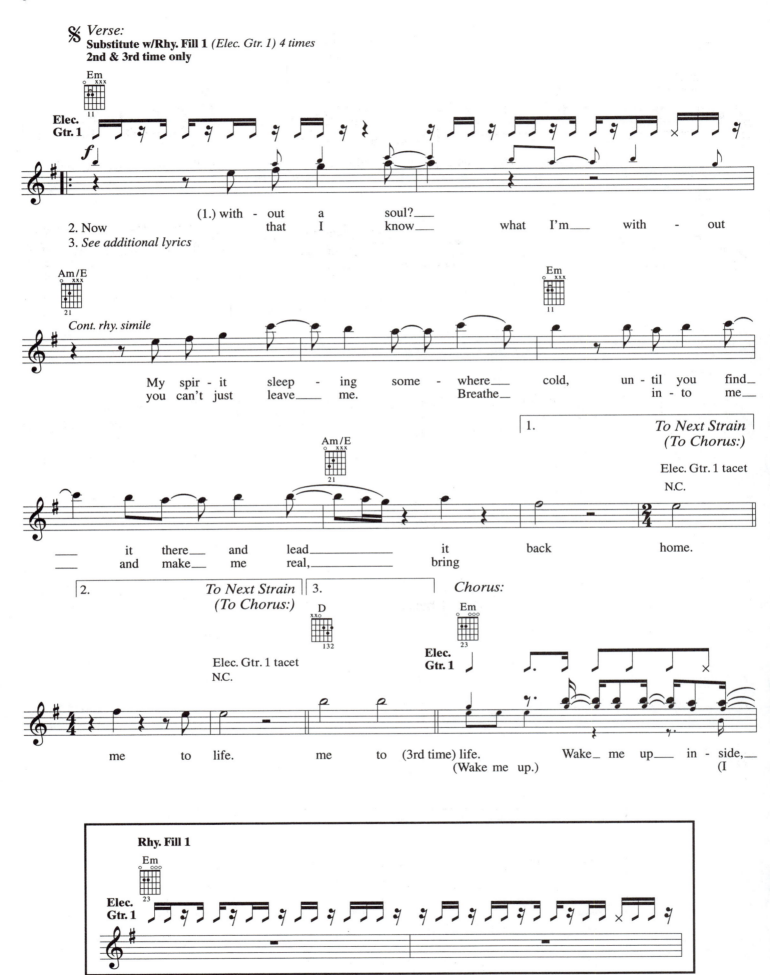

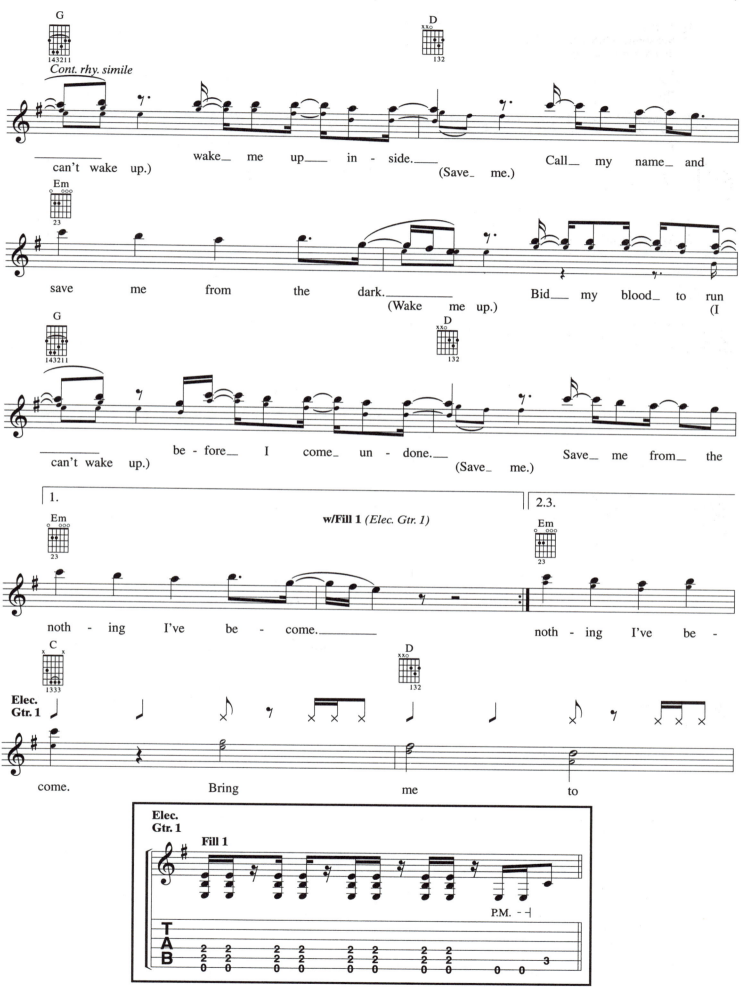

8

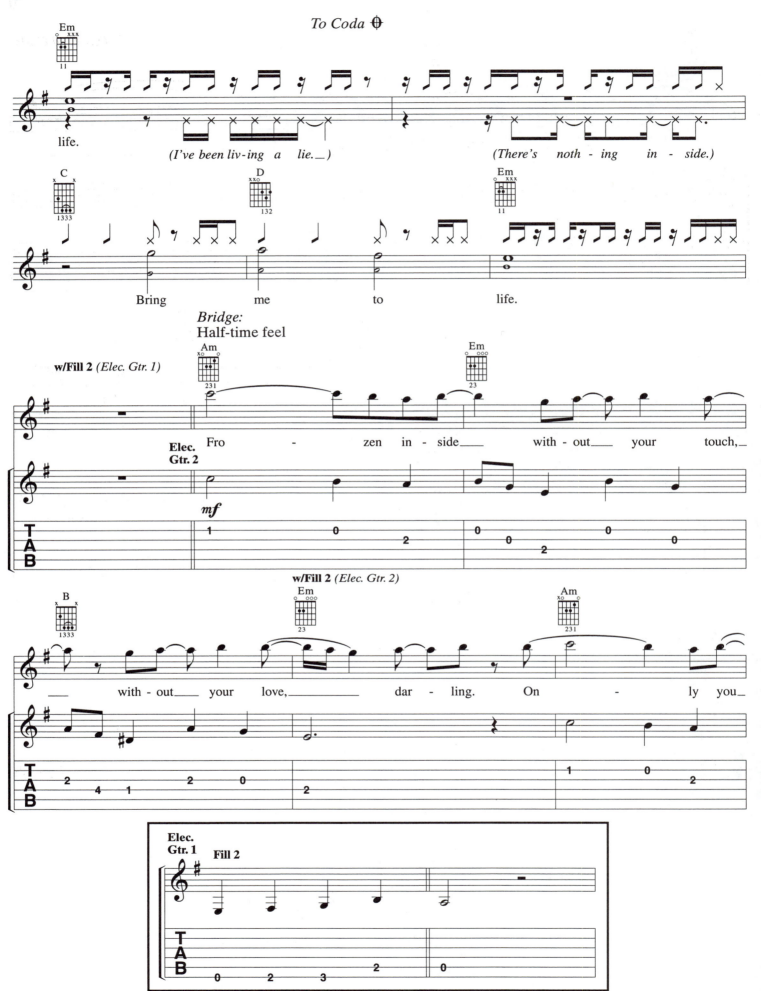

Bring Me to Life - 5 - 4
PGM0314

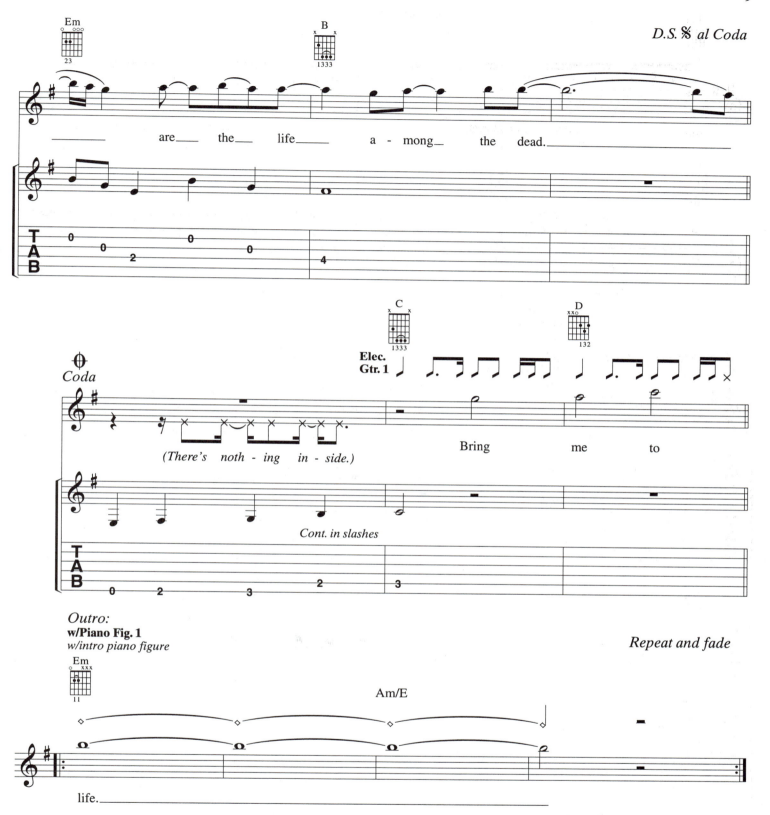

Verse 3:
All this time I can't believe I couldn't see.
Kept in the dark, but you were there in front of me.
I've been sleeping a thousand years, it seems.
Got to open my eyes to everything.
Without a thought, without a voice, without a soul,
Don't let me die here.
There must be something more.
Bring me to life.
(To Chorus:)

GOING UNDER

Elec. Gtr. 1 tuned:
⑥ = B   ③ = D
⑤ = E   ② = G
④ = A   ① = B

Written by Ben Moody,
Amy Lee and David Hodges

Moderately ♩ = 84
Verse 1:
B5

Elec. Gtr. 1   *Cont. rhy. simile*

Now I will tell you what I've done for you.

Fif - ty thou - sand tears I've cried.

w/Piano Fill 1

Scream - ing, de - ceiv - ing and bleed - ing for you, and

Elec. Gtr. 1 tacet
G

you still won't hear me (...go - ing un - der.)

Verses 2 & 3:
B5

Resume rhy. fig. simile

2. Don't want your hand this time. I'll save my - self.
3. Blur - ring and stir - ring the truth and the lies

Piano Fill 1
Piano

EVERYBODY'S FOOL

Acous. Gtr. in DADGAD tuning:
⑥ = D   ③ = G
⑤ = A   ② = A
④ = D   ① = D

Elec Gtr. in Drop D tuning: ⑥ = D

Written by Ben Moody,
Amy Lee and David Hodges

Moderately ♩ = 92

Intro:

*Chords implied by orchestration.

16

Everybody's Fool - 5 - 3
PGM0314

MY IMMORTAL

Written by Ben Moody,
Amy Lee and David Hodges

Slowly and freely ♩ = 80

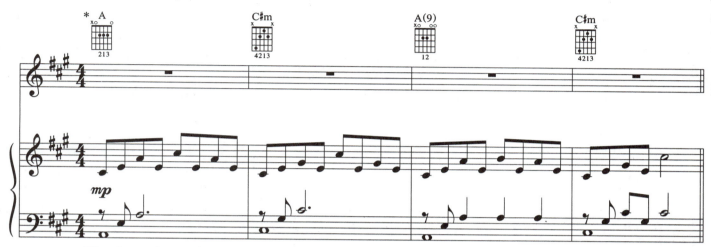

*There is no guitar on this recording. Chords frames indicate suggested guitar chords only.

Verse:

1. I'm so tired of be - ing here,___ sup - pressed___ by all___ my child - ish fears._____ And if you have to leave,___

Verse 2:
You used to captivate me
By your resonating light.
But, now I'm bound by the life you left behind.
Your face, it haunts
My once pleasant dreams.
Your voice, it chased away
All the sanity in me.
These wounds won't seem to heal.
This pain is just too real.
There's just too much that time can not erase.
(To Chorus:)

HAUNTED

All gtrs. in Drop D tuning:
⑥ = D

Written by Ben Moody,
Amy Lee and David Hodges

Moderately slow ♩ = 76

*Elec. Gtr. Verse 2 only.

1. Long lost words whis-per slow-ly to me.
2. Hunt - ing you, I can smell you a - live.

Still can't find what keeps me here.
Your heart pound - ing in my head.

1. When all this time I've been so hol-
- low in - side. (I know you're still there.)

To Next Strain
(To Chorus:)

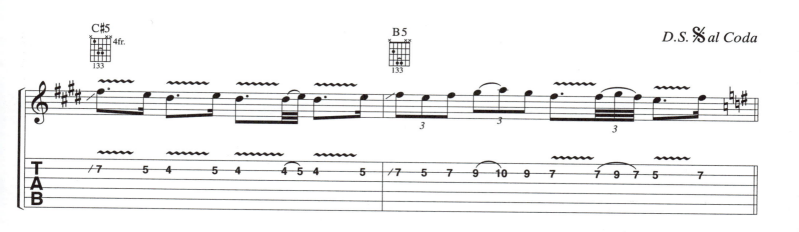

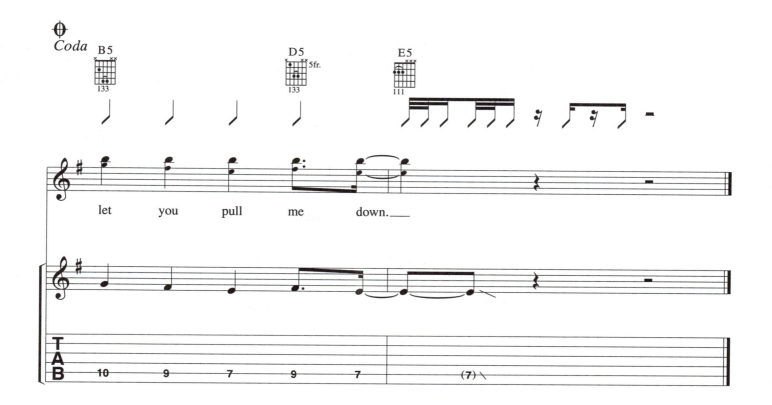

TOURNIQUET

Written by
Ben Moody, Amy Lee,
David Hodges and William Rocky Gray

IMAGINARY

Elec. Gtr. 1 tuned:
⑥ = B ③ = D
⑤ = E ② = G
④ = A ① = B

Written by Ben Moody,
Amy Lee and David Hodges

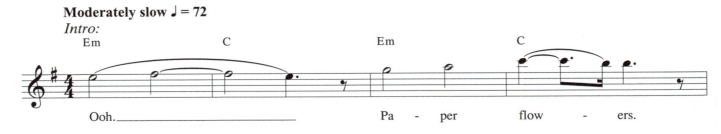

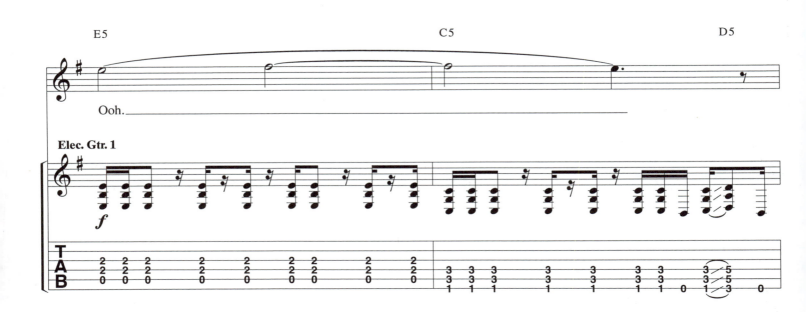

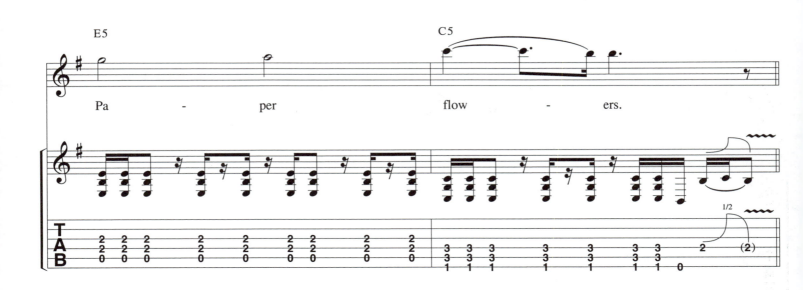

34

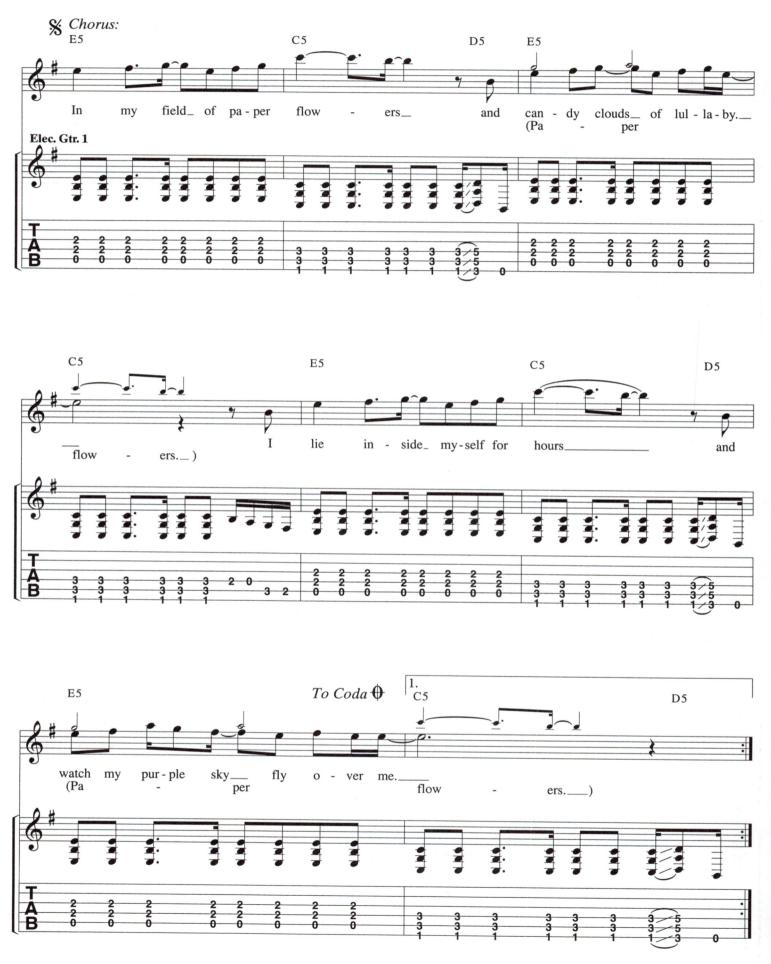

Imaginary - 6 - 3
PGM0314

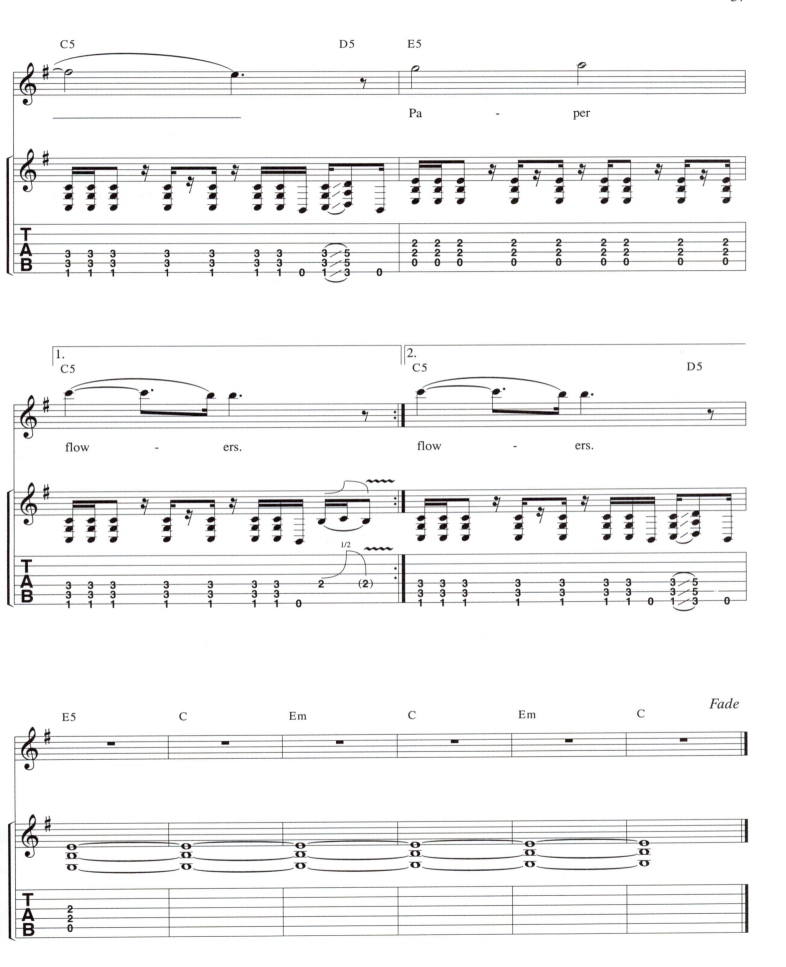

TAKING OVER ME

Written by
Ben Moody, Amy Lee,
David Hodges and John LeCompt

Elec. Gtr. 1 tuned:
⑥ = A   ③ = D
⑤ = E   ② = G
④ = A   ① = B

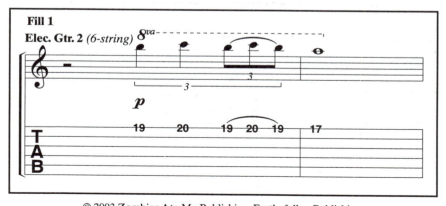

Fill 1
Elec. Gtr. 2 (6-string)

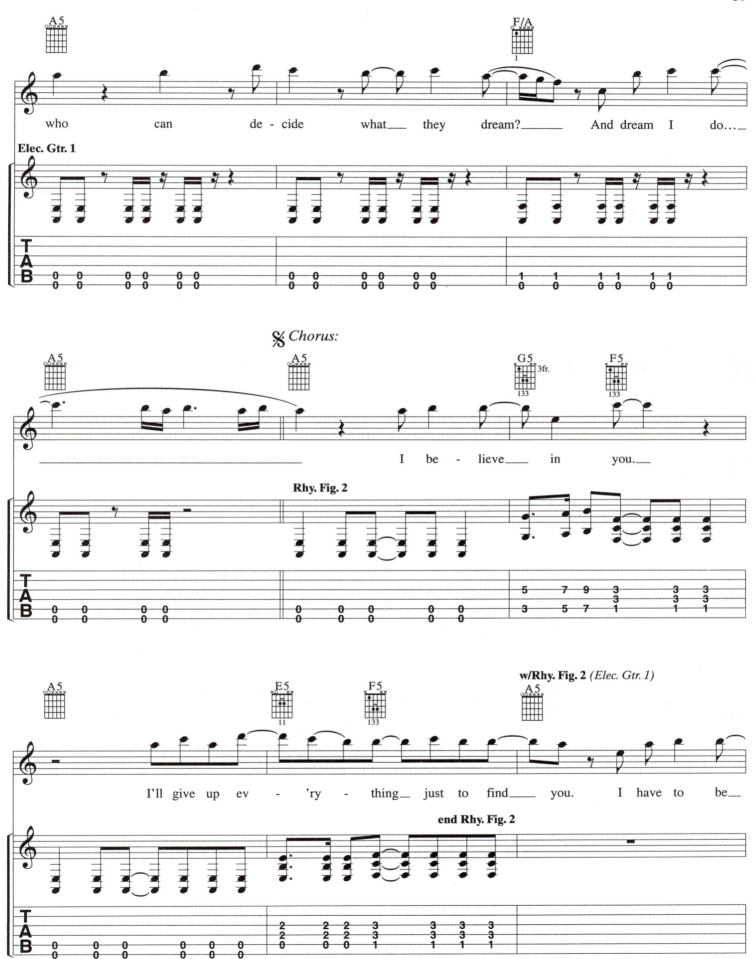

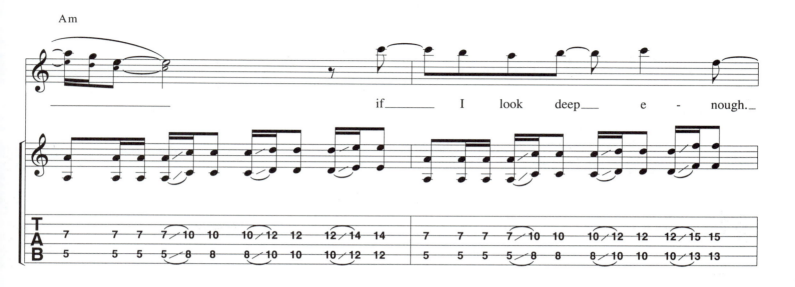

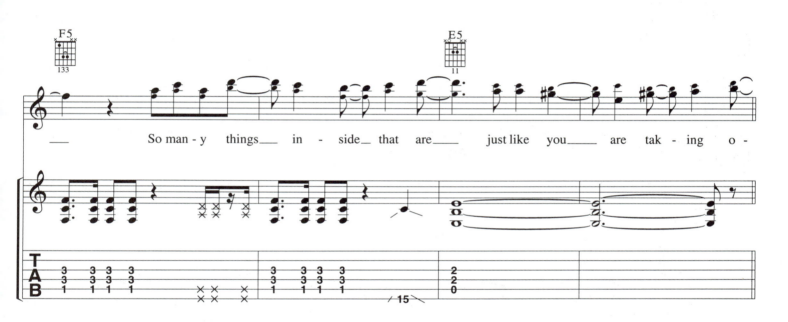

HELLO

Written by Ben Moody,
Amy Lee and David Hodges

Slowly, with expression ♩ = 72

(with pedal)

Verse:

1. Play - ground school bell
2. If I smile and

rings a - gain.___
don't be - lieve.___

* There is no guitar on this recording. Chord frames indicate suggested guitar chords only.

Hello - 5 - 1
PGM0314

46

Hello - 5 - 4
PGM0314

MY LAST BREATH

Written by Ben Moody,
Amy Lee and David Hodges

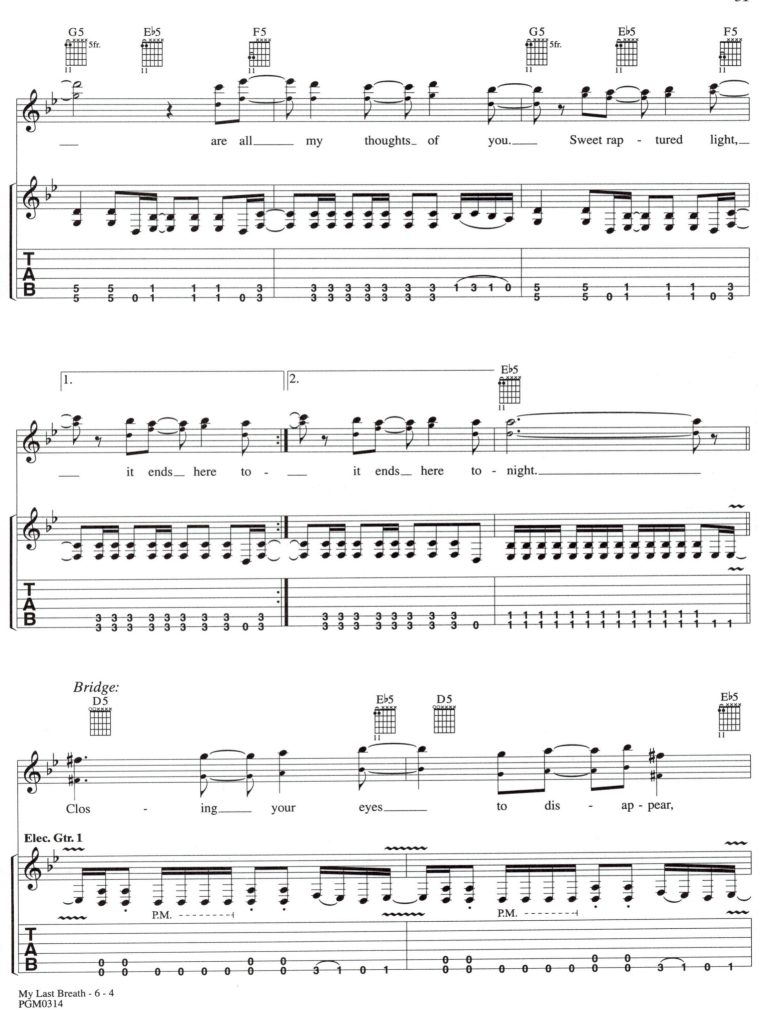

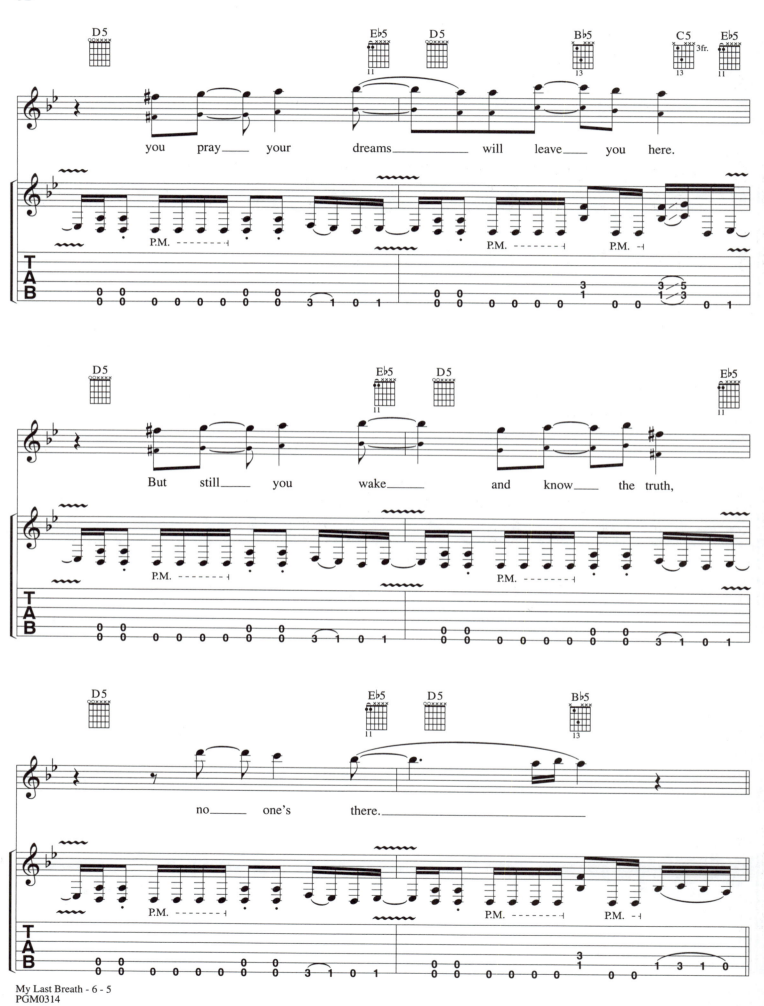

Chorus:

Say good - night, don't be___ a - fraid.

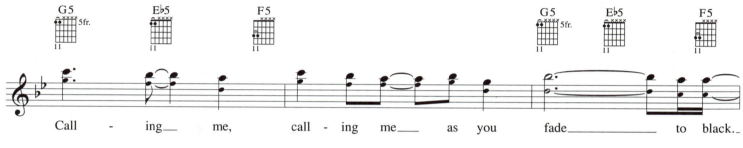

Call - ing___ me, call - ing me___ as you fade_____ to black.__

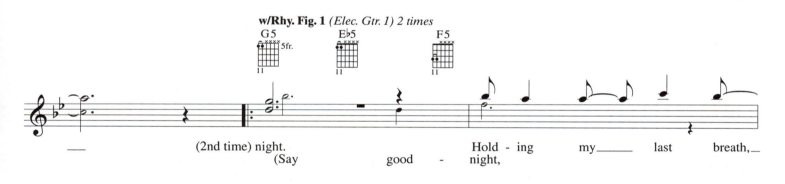

___ (2nd time) night. (Say good - night, Hold - ing my___ last breath,__

___ don't be___ a - fraid.) safe in - side___ my - self___ are all___ (Call - ing___ me,

___ my thoughts___ of you.___ Sweet rap - tured light,___ it ends___ here to -
call - ing___ me.)

Repeat till fade

My Last Breath - 6 - 6
PGM0314

WHISPER

Written by Ben Moody,
Amy Lee and David Hodges

All gtrs. in Drop D tuning:
⑥ = D

Moderately ♩ = 84

Intro:

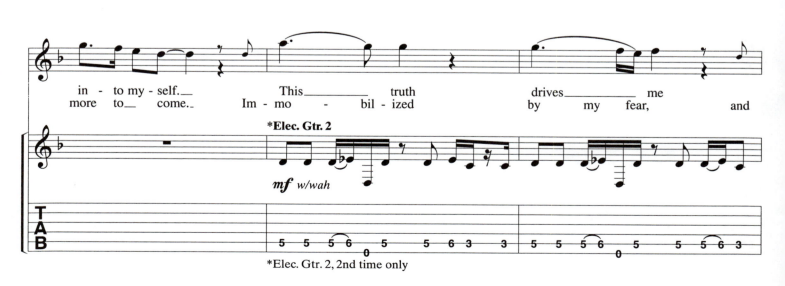

Verse:
Elec. Gtr. 1 tacet

1. Catch me   as I   fall,__   say you're here__ and it's all   o - ver__ now.__

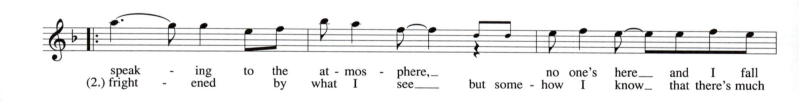

speak - ing   to the   at - mos - phere,   no one's here__ and I   fall
(2.) fright - ened   by what I   see____   but some - how I   know__ that there's much

in - to my - self.__   This_____   truth   drives_____ me
more to__ come.__   Im - mo - bil - ized   by   my   fear,   and

*Elec. Gtr. 2

mf w/wah

*Elec. Gtr. 2, 2nd time only

w/Rhy. Fig. 2 *(Elec. Gtr. 1)*

E5 F5 E5   F5 G5   D5 Bb5 C5   D5

though they're scream - ing__ your name.__)   Don't close your eyes.   (God knows what lies__ be - hind

Bb5   G5   *To Coda* ⊕   **1.** E5 F5 E5   F5 G5

Don't   turn   out   the   light.__   nev - er sleep, nev - er die.__

w/Rhy. Fig. 1 *(Elec. Gtr. 1)*   **2.** E5 F5 E5   F5 G5
Dm

__ them,

__)   2. I'm   __   nev - er sleep, nev - er die.)

Bridge:
Dm   C/E

Fall - en an - gels at__ my feet,__   whis - pered voic - es at__ my ear.__

Elec. Gtr. 3

Gm   Dm

Death be - fore__ my eyes,__   ly - ing next__ to me__ I fear.__   She

beck - ons me__ shall I__ give in?__ Up - on my end__ shall I__ be - gin__ for -

sak - ing all__ I've fall - en for__ I rise__ to meet__ the end?__

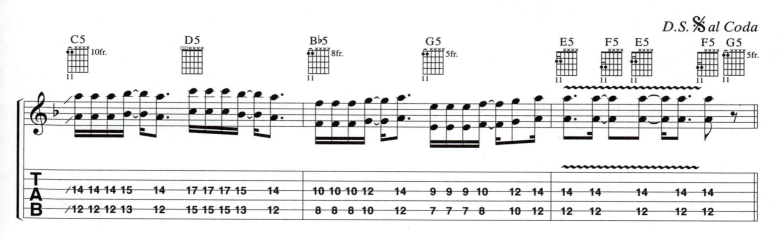

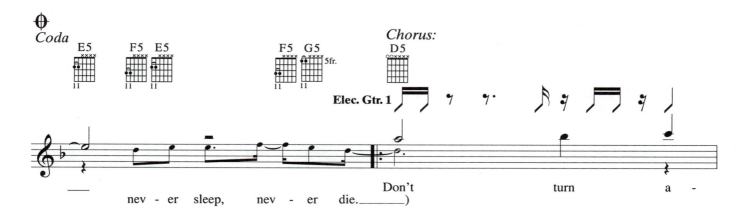

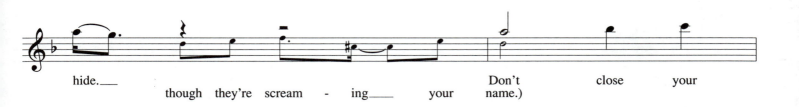

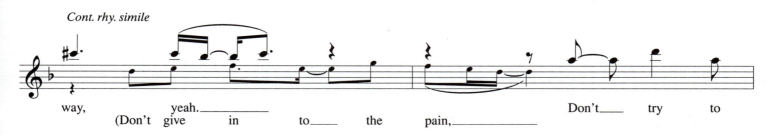

GOING UNDER

NOW I WILL TELL YOU WHAT I'VE DONE FOR YOU
50 THOUSAND TEARS I'VE CRIED
SCREAMING DECEIVING AND BLEEDING FOR YOU
AND YOU STILL WON'T HEAR ME
DON'T WANT YOUR HAND THIS TIME I'LL SAVE MYSELF
MAYBE I'LL WAKE UP FOR ONCE
NOT TORMENTED DAILY DEFEATED BY YOU
JUST WHEN I THOUGHT I'D REACHED THE BOTTOM
I'M DYING AGAIN

I'M GOING UNDER
DROWNING IN YOU
I'M FALLING FOREVER
I'VE GOT TO BREAK THROUGH
I'M GOING UNDER

BLURRING AND STIRRING THE TRUTH AND THE LIES
SO I DON'T KNOW WHAT'S REAL AND WHAT'S NOT
ALWAYS CONFUSING THE THOUGHTS IN MY HEAD
SO I CAN'T TRUST MYSELF ANYMORE
I'M DYING AGAIN

I'M GOING UNDER
DROWNING IN YOU
I'M FALLING FOREVER
I'VE GOT TO BREAK THROUGH

SO GO ON AND SCREAM
SCREAM AT ME I'M SO FAR AWAY
I WON'T BE BROKEN AGAIN
I'VE GOT TO BREATHE I CAN'T KEEP GOING UNDER

BRING ME TO LIFE

HOW CAN YOU SEE INTO MY EYES LIKE OPEN DOORS
LEADING YOU DOWN INTO MY CORE
WHERE I'VE BECOME SO NUMB WITHOUT A SOUL
MY SPIRIT SLEEPING SOMEWHERE COLD
UNTIL YOU FIND IT THERE AND LEAD IT BACK HOME

WAKE ME UP INSIDE
WAKE ME UP INSIDE
CALL MY NAME AND SAVE ME FROM THE DARK
BID MY BLOOD TO RUN BEFORE I COME UNDONE
SAVE ME FROM THE NOTHING I'VE BECOME

NOW THAT I KNOW WHAT I'M WITHOUT
YOU CAN'T JUST LEAVE ME
BREATHE INTO ME AND MAKE ME REAL
BRING ME TO LIFE

WAKE ME UP INSIDE
WAKE ME UP INSIDE
CALL MY NAME AND SAVE ME FROM THE DARK
BID MY BLOOD TO RUN BEFORE I COME UNDONE
SAVE ME FROM THE NOTHING I'VE BECOME
BRING ME TO LIFE

FROZEN INSIDE WITHOUT YOUR TOUCH WITHOUT YOUR LOVE
DARLING ONLY YOU ARE THE LIFE AMONG THE DEAD

ALL THIS TIME I CAN'T BELIEVE I COULDN'T SEE
KEPT IN THE DARK BUT YOU WERE THERE IN FRONT OF ME
I'VE BEEN SLEEPING A THOUSAND YEARS IT SEEMS
GOT TO OPEN MY EYES TO EVERYTHING
WITHOUT A THOUGHT WITHOUT A VOICE WITHOUT A SOUL
DON'T LET ME DIE HERE THERE MUST BE SOMETHING MORE
BRING ME TO LIFE

EVERYBODY'S FOOL

PERFECT BY NATURE
ICONS OF SELF INDULGENCE
JUST WHAT WE ALL NEED
MORE LIES ABOUT A WORLD THAT

NEVER WAS AND NEVER WILL BE
YOU DON'T KNOW HOW YOU'VE BETRAYED ME
AND SOMEHOW YOU'VE GOT EVERYBODY FOOLED

NEVER WAS AND NEVER WILL BE
HAVE YOU NO SHAME DON'T YOU SEE ME
YOU KNOW YOU'VE GOT EVERYBODY FOOLED

WITHOUT THE MASK WHERE WILL YOU HIDE
CAN'T FIND YOURSELF LOST IN YOUR LIE

I KNOW THE TRUTH NOW
I KNOW WHO YOU ARE
AND I DON'T LOVE YOU ANYMORE

LOOK HERE SHE COMES NOW
BOW DOWN AND STARE IN WONDER
OH HOW WE LOVE YOU
NO FLAWS WHEN YOU'RE PRETENDING
BUT NOW I KNOW SHE

IT NEVER WAS AND NEVER WILL BE
YOU'RE NOT REAL AND YOU CAN'T SAVE ME
SOMEHOW NOW YOU'RE EVERYBODY'S FOOL

My Immortal

I'M SO TIRED OF BEING HERE
SUPPRESSED BY ALL OF MY CHILDISH FEARS
AND IF YOU HAVE TO LEAVE
I WISH THAT YOU WOULD JUST LEAVE
BECAUSE YOUR PRESENCE STILL LINGERS HERE
AND IT WON'T LEAVE ME ALONE

YOU USED TO CAPTIVATE ME
BY YOUR RESONATING LIGHT
BUT NOW I'M BOUND BY THE LIFE YOU LEFT BEHIND
YOUR FACE IT HAUNTS MY ONCE PLEASANT DREAMS
YOUR VOICE IT CHASED AWAY ALL THE SANITY IN ME

THESE WOUNDS WON'T SEEM TO HEAL
THIS PAIN IS JUST TOO REAL
THERE'S JUST TOO MUCH THAT TIME CANNOT ERASE

THESE WOUNDS WON'T SEEM TO HEAL
THIS PAIN IS JUST TOO REAL
THERE'S JUST TOO MUCH THAT TIME CANNOT ERASE

WHEN YOU CRIED I'D WIPE AWAY ALL OF YOUR TEARS
WHEN YOU'D SCREAM I'D FIGHT AWAY ALL OF YOUR FEARS
AND I'VE HELD YOUR HAND THROUGH ALL OF THESE YEARS
BUT YOU STILL HAVE ALL OF ME

WHEN YOU CRIED I'D WIPE AWAY ALL OF YOUR TEARS
WHEN YOU'D SCREAM I'D FIGHT AWAY ALL OF YOUR FEARS
AND I'VE HELD YOUR HAND THROUGH ALL OF THESE YEARS
BUT YOU STILL HAVE ALL OF ME

I'VE TRIED SO HARD TO TELL MYSELF THAT YOU'RE GONE
AND THOUGH YOU'RE STILL WITH ME
I'VE BEEN ALONE ALL ALONG

Haunted

LONG LOST WORDS WHISPER SLOWLY TO ME
STILL CAN'T FIND WHAT KEEPS ME HERE
WHEN ALL THIS TIME I'VE BEEN SO HOLLOW INSIDE
I KNOW YOU'RE STILL THERE

HUNTING YOU I CAN SMELL YOU - ALIVE
YOUR HEART POUNDING IN MY HEAD

WATCHING ME WANTING ME
I CAN FEEL YOU PULL ME DOWN
SAVING ME RAPING ME
WATCHING ME

WATCHING ME WANTING ME
I CAN FEEL YOU PULL ME DOWN
FEARING YOU LOVING YOU
I WON'T LET YOU PULL ME DOWN

Tourniquet

I TRIED TO KILL THE PAIN
BUT ONLY BROUGHT MORE
I LAY DYING
AND I'M POURING CRIMSON REGRET AND BETRAYAL
I'M DYING PRAYING BLEEDING AND SCREAMING
AM I TOO LOST TO BE SAVED
AM I TOO LOST?

WILL YOU BE ON THE OTHER SIDE
OR WILL YOU FORGET ME
I'M DYING PRAYING BLEEDING AND SCREAMING
AM I TOO LOST TO BE SAVED
AM I TOO LOST?

MY GOD MY TOURNIQUET
RETURN TO ME SALVATION
MY GOD MY TOURNIQUET
RETURN TO ME SALVATION

MY GOD MY TOURNIQUET
RETURN TO ME SALVATION
MY GOD MY TOURNIQUET
RETURN TO ME SALVATION

MY WOUNDS CRY FOR THE GRAVE
MY SOUL CRIES FOR DELIVERANCE
WILL I BE DENIED CHRIST
TOURNIQUET
MY SUICIDE

DO YOU REMEMBER ME
LOST FOR SO LONG

IMAGINARY

I LINGER IN THE DOORWAY
OF ALARM CLOCK SCREAMING
MONSTERS CALLING MY NAME
LET ME STAY
WHERE THE WIND WILL WHISPER TO ME
WHERE THE RAINDROPS
AS THEY'RE FALLING TELL A STORY

IN MY FIELD OF PAPER FLOWERS
AND CANDY CLOUDS OF LULLABY
I LIE INSIDE MYSELF FOR HOURS
AND WATCH MY PURPLE SKY FLY OVER ME

DON'T SAY I'M OUT OF TOUCH
WITH THIS RAMPANT CHAOS - YOUR REALITY
I KNOW WELL WHAT LIES BEYOND MY SLEEPING REFUGE
THE NIGHTMARE I BUILT MY OWN WORLD TO ESCAPE

IN MY FIELD OF PAPER FLOWERS
AND CANDY CLOUDS OF LULLABY
I LIE INSIDE MYSELF FOR HOURS
AND WATCH MY PURPLE SKY FLY OVER ME

SWALLOWED UP IN THE SOUND OF MY SCREAMING
CANNOT CEASE FOR THE FEAR OF SILENT NIGHTS
OH HOW I LONG FOR THE DEEP SLEEP DREAMING
THE GODDESS OF IMAGINARY LIGHT

TAKING OVER ME

YOU DON'T REMEMBER ME
BUT I REMEMBER YOU
I LIE AWAKE AND TRY SO HARD
NOT TO THINK OF YOU
BUT WHO CAN DECIDE WHAT THEY DREAM?
AND DREAM I DO...

I BELIEVE IN YOU
I'LL GIVE UP EVERYTHING JUST TO FIND YOU
I HAVE TO BE WITH YOU TO LIVE TO BREATHE
YOU'RE TAKING OVER ME

HAVE YOU FORGOTTEN ALL I KNOW
AND ALL WE HAD?

YOU SAW ME MOURNING MY LOVE FOR YOU
AND TOUCHED MY HAND
I KNEW YOU LOVED ME THEN

I BELIEVE IN YOU
I'LL GIVE UP EVERYTHING JUST TO FIND YOU
I HAVE TO BE WITH YOU TO LIVE TO BREATHE
YOU'RE TAKING OVER ME

I LOOK IN THE MIRROR AND SEE YOUR FACE
IF I LOOK DEEP ENOUGH
SO MANY THINGS INSIDE THAT ARE
JUST LIKE YOU ARE TAKING OVER

HELLO

PLAYGROUND SCHOOL BELL RINGS AGAIN
RAIN CLOUDS COME TO PLAY AGAIN
HAS NO ONE TOLD YOU SHE'S NOT BREATHING?
HELLO I'M YOUR MIND GIVING YOU
SOMEONE TO TALK TO
HELLO

IF I SMILE AND DON'T BELIEVE
SOON I KNOW I'LL WAKE FROM THIS DREAM

DON'T TRY TO FIX ME I'M NOT BROKEN
HELLO I'M THE LIE LIVING FOR YOU SO YOU CAN HIDE
DON'T CRY

SUDDENLY I KNOW I'M NOT SLEEPING
HELLO I'M STILL HERE
ALL THAT'S LEFT OF YESTERDAY

MY LAST BREATH

HOLD ON TO ME LOVE
YOU KNOW I CAN'T STAY LONG
ALL I WANTED TO SAY WAS I LOVE YOU AND I'M NOT AFRAID
CAN YOU HEAR ME?
CAN YOU FEEL ME IN YOUR ARMS?

I KNOW YOU HEAR ME
I CAN TASTE IT IN YOUR TEARS

HOLDING MY LAST BREATH
SAFE INSIDE MYSELF
ARE ALL MY THOUGHTS OF YOU
SWEET RAPTURED LIGHT
IT ENDS HERE TONIGHT

HOLDING MY LAST BREATH
SAFE INSIDE MYSELF
ARE ALL MY THOUGHTS OF YOU
SWEET RAPTURED LIGHT
IT ENDS HERE TONIGHT

CLOSING YOUR EYES TO DISAPPEAR
YOU PRAY YOUR DREAMS WILL LEAVE YOU HERE
BUT STILL YOU WAKE AND KNOW THE TRUTH
NO ONE'S THERE

I'LL MISS THE WINTER
A WORLD OF FRAGILE THINGS
LOOK FOR ME IN THE WHITE FOREST
HIDING IN A HOLLOW TREE (COME FIND ME)

SAY GOODNIGHT
DON'T BE AFRAID
CALLING ME CALLING ME AS YOU FADE TO BLACK

WHISPER

CATCH ME AS I FALL
SAY YOU'RE HERE AND IT'S ALL OVER NOW
SPEAKING TO THE ATMOSPHERE
NO ONE'S HERE AND I FALL INTO MYSELF
THIS TRUTH DRIVES ME INTO MADNESS
I KNOW I CAN STOP THE PAIN IF I WILL IT ALL AWAY

AND SOON TO BE BLINDED BY TEARS
I CAN STOP THE PAIN IF I WILL IT ALL AWAY

DON'T TURN AWAY
DON'T GIVE IN TO THE PAIN
DON'T TRY TO HIDE
THOUGH THEY'RE SCREAMING YOUR NAME
DON'T CLOSE YOUR EYES
GOD KNOWS WHAT LIES BEHIND THEM
DON'T TURN OUT THE LIGHT
NEVER SLEEP NEVER DIE

DON'T TURN AWAY
DON'T GIVE IN TO THE PAIN
DON'T TRY TO HIDE
THOUGH THEY'RE SCREAMING YOUR NAME
DON'T CLOSE YOUR EYES
GOD KNOWS WHAT LIES BEHIND THEM
DON'T TURN OUT THE LIGHT
NEVER SLEEP NEVER DIE

FALLEN ANGELS AT MY FEET
WHISPERED VOICES AT MY EAR
DEATH BEFORE MY EYES
LYING NEXT TO ME I FEAR
SHE BECKONS ME SHALL I GIVE IN
UPON MY END SHALL I BEGIN
FORSAKING ALL I'VE FALLEN FOR I RISE TO MEET THE END

I'M FRIGHTENED BY WHAT I SEE
BUT SOMEHOW I KNOW THAT THERE'S MUCH MORE TO COME
IMMOBILIZED BY MY FEAR